Exceptional
BLOOM

FLOURISHING IN
THE NEXT SEASON

PAULA MASTERS

ISBN: 978-1-7377427-2-2

Editing Consultant: Michelle Shelfer, benediction.biz

Published by FarmHousePress

Contents

Introduction

Someone wisely stated once that the only thing certain about life is its uncertainty. There is no getting around it—life is always changing, and change can be painful. But what we may not have realized is the sacred opportunity *change* presents. Beyond the sadness and confusion that often accompany transition lies an invitation to enter into a new season filled with peace and deep assurance.

With this said, let me tell you what this book is not about. It is not about menopause. In fact, I never mention the word in this book except for just now to let you know that it's not in here! Also, this book is not about fluffy, silly, girly things. There definitely is some pink involved, but not the kind that conveys the conflicting messages of princess gowns and girl power.

What this book *does* discuss are the difficult and challenging transitional stages we women go through as we move from one phase of life to the next. This can include any kind of change: from being a mom with children at home to having an empty nest; from being married to being divorced; from having a career change to ending a career altogether; from good health to experiencing health issues; from taking care of an elderly parent to coping with the death of that loved one. Although change can happen at any time, life demonstrates that a concentrated amount of change happens the further we advance in years. And while many writings center on positive thinking in these areas, they often serve as temporary bandages for the heartaches that coincide with these seasons. Oh, how our hearts need more!

Exceptional Bloom sets out to deliver the "more" our hearts yearn for. Leading us step by step to the rich season of soul-flourishing, each chapter builds upon the previous one, offering both sanctuary and spiritual direction. Digging deep into the Bible, we discover a treasure that is often hidden in the difficult process. For the woman who is going through a major life change, if there was ever a time to find that treasure, this would be it.

You will feel the freedom to be open about issues that bring both pain and joy. You will also be encouraged not to give up as the various doors of life close, nor to downplay the heartache involved.

There is a new door open—one of great discovery to the soul. Yours is a heavenly season, one that is filled with hope and grace—a time that binds you to others on the same path with a common experience. You will find a wonderful sisterhood.

Welcome to the exceptional bloom, flourishing in the next season!

1

Casting the Vision

*H*ave you wondered if your heart was destined for endless days of gray? If so, you are not alone. Disappointments that naturally come as life changes can cast what feels like a never-ending shadow of nightfall across our souls. Clouds of discouragement that form in seasons of transition predict climates of gloom. And like the absence of sunlit skies, hope often seems elusive during these times.

Interestingly, this mental phenomenon is comparable to the clinical mechanics of seasonal depression, a condition brought on annually by lack of sunlight. Studies show that when gray atmosphere blankets the sky for long durations, serotonin levels in a person's brain can drop, interfering with the neurotransmitters that affect mood. In essence—the same way that the brain needs sunlight, the heart needs the illumination of *real* hope, not only to help navigate difficult transitions but to wonderfully thrive in the next season.

With this in mind, I want to share something that might shock and surprise you. You are actually standing on the cusp of an extraordinary time! Daybreak is on the horizon, and the dawning of a soft shade of pink is waiting to set your heart aglow. The best way I can describe this experience is to call it the season of exceptional bloom, which is why I chose that for the title of this book. I love these words because they capture the hope of how your life is about to open up (if you allow it) into a unique and beautiful blooming that is far from ordinary in any sense of the word.

But first, we must cast a vision of what this means.

Imagine for a moment coming upon the most glorious of prospects, where the purposes of your past merge with God's specific plan for your future—where the original blueprint of "you" takes on a whole new meaning. I am not suggesting a replication of your former days but rather your history becoming the springboard for something entirely different and new.

Let me give you an example. I live in Florida, where the typical home has a few common features: lawns, palm trees, and swimming pools. But not ours—our house is an anomaly to this region. Fifty years ago, the original owners had coral rock imported to create sweeping waterfalls that encompassed the entire length of the backyard. I'm sure it was very enchanting when newly built, but by the time the house came across our path, it was a different story. Broken down and overrun with weeds, the house was an eyesore to the entire neighborhood.

We found this house when we were looking into buying a foreclosure. Our children were grown, so my husband and I decided to buy a home with interesting structure and origin. It was obvious that the original plan for this home was a creative venture at one point, so, being intrigued with its initial design, we bought it. We were also excited about our freedom to turn it into something new and fantastic—and perhaps even add a little "Florida" to it.

We replaced the original terrazzo flooring with coastal wood to give it a sense of warmth. We knocked out one of the kitchen walls to give the room a more spacious feel. We replaced all of the windows and sliders with double-paned hurricane-impact glass. This rickety old house began its journey of becoming rejuvenated, new, and in many ways better and stronger than ever.

We didn't replicate history; we used the house's past as a springboard for something wonderfully new.

Coincidentally, during the purchasing phase, while surveying the backyard, I came across a bromeliad blooming in the shade of our banyan tree. Bromeliads are plants that store water in their leaves as a means to nourish themselves. I was fascinated to see that even with the neglect of the property over the years, God had provided this plant with exactly what it needed not only to flourish but to bloom magnificently even in the worst of conditions. There it was—a lovely shade of pink in the midst of a gray, dull landscape. As I gazed upon its beauty, I couldn't help thinking there was a parallel here—not only in the rejuvenation of an old house that most thought had seen its day, but also in the discovery of the bloom of the bromeliad.

Surely, as women, we too come into a gray season when we feel run down from the years, tired, and somewhat saddened that the days of our youth have seen their end. So many changes and transitions—the things we poured our life's energy into—no longer need our energy. Hours of personal investment are swept away in the tide of years. Our children have grown, our ambitions have waned, our bodies have changed, and even our stamina levels are different. Yet, just like the bromeliad plant, we have a God-given capacity, even now, for blooming—and producing not just any ordinary bloom but one with unique qualities. But what does that look like?

When my husband and I cast a vision for the old house, we had to intentionally project what kind of life might fill its walls. Whatever its previous function had been, all would change shortly. We imagined the possibilities. We visualized the grandkids playing in the house and the special room we would create just for them. We envisioned a fire pit outside set amidst lush landscape, surrounded by the laughter and fun of our family. We would share Christmases with close friends as we sat around our spacious living room, mugs of spiced apple cider in hand. The more we thought about it, the more we became delighted with our ideas of what the home would become.

For those of us experiencing life-changing transition, casting the vision for our exceptional blooming is just as important, but it does not happen so easily. It takes effort because we feel drained. Projecting all life's potential can be difficult if change catches us by surprise. To top it all off, many times we are not even sure who we are anymore, and an identity crisis sets in (transition has a way of doing this). We become discouraged instead of delighted. In fact, we can even feel immobilized by change. So, there it sits—this exceptional season of our lives—unopened like a large gift package in the corner, and we are perplexed at what to do with it.

Yet, as disorienting as this experience may feel, we need to know that this time of life does not catch God by surprise. He has foreseen this slice of our existence and already has it in mind. In fact, He has specific plans to nourish and cultivate it. Realizing God's forethought about my well-being in a time of transition was a game changer for me.

Psalm 139:13–16 highlights this reality. Well known for displaying God's intimacy with us in our beginnings, this passage also reveals God's loving hand in all our seasons of life.

For You created my inmost being; You knit me together in my mother's womb. I praise You because I am fearfully and wonderfully made; Your works are wonderful, I know that full well. My frame was not hidden from You when I was made in the secret place, when I was woven together in the depths of the earth. Your eyes saw my unformed body; all the days ordained for me were written in Your book before one of them came to be.

Notice the Scripture says that *all* of our days were written long ago—before even one of them came to be—and God already has seen them. We might have thought the prime of our lives was a time now past, like our youth. But God sees our prime as something entirely different. He is interested in the whole picture—the *all* of our lives. Transition and change make way for that which otherwise would not be. The second half of our lives yields new opportunities that were not available in the first half. In other words, we see our days in terms of what we perceive as our prime, but God sees our days as being unlimited. He sees that we are free to venture beyond our perceived limitations.

This time in our lives is a new territory beyond the boundaries of what we are familiar with, so it feels foreign—yet it is not outside the boundaries of God's plans for us. We may have come to this stage of life wondering if we were at the end, destined for nothing but a dismal future, but the reality is that we are at the beginning of a season that is quite unique. Up until this point, life may have consumed us. Now we are at the turning point of becoming a consumer of a different kind of life altogether.

Here's what I mean. When we are young, we are driven by our hopes and dreams of what life should be. We put a lot of effort toward achieving those expectations. Yet, now, as we look at our lives circumspectly, we realize that even though God has used those aspirations to mold us into the women we've become, He never intended for us to be defined by our hopes and dreams (or failures). In fact, now that we are released from their obligations of priority, we are free to look at life from a new perspective.

Honestly, I marvel at the things I used to think were so important but that now have lost their hold. For instance, after my mother died, I was deeply grieved. Missing her caring ways, I searched for an older woman who might be a maternal voice in my life. I was on a mission, eager to find someone who would take a genuine interest in me as my mother did. I looked high and low. I eventually met a woman at our church mature in age, who invited me to lunch. I remember thinking, *It's finally happening!* I discovered soon after my arrival, however, that she had invited me over to share some family issues, and she was seeking *my* advice. Although I highly valued our conversations, I still remember feeling the void of my pursuit. I continued my quest, but my mentors ended up being books and people I would never meet.

That goal was a part of my *perceived* prime. Now that sense of urgency has long since passed and is no longer on my radar. Its hold has released with the passage of time, and there has been a great shift in my outlook. Finding its end simply meant a new beginning—one without that particular expectation. It was so important to me—and then it no longer was. I believe God gave me poverty in this area so that I could better understand how important it is to be that listening ear for others.

My life has taken a new view from this one change in perspective. The season of the exceptional bloom yields a surprising exploration into many of these types of changes that are freeing and new. We are no longer bound to the old, limited ideas from what we thought was our prime. We are free to move forward and flourish in a new way.

You see, we are not the same people we were in our younger days. Those years were a part of shaping who we are in this season of blooming. As we dig deeper into what that blooming looks like, we will find ourselves on a journey of intense transformation. We need to know it's not only okay to travel to this place in the heart but that God has been expecting us to make the journey all along. He is here awaiting us with welcoming arms. He will not leave us to bump around in the dark but will lead us every step of the way into in-depth discoveries we may never have realized were possible when we were younger.

In light of this truth, life that comes after change and transition is certainly an exceptional time to bloom. Dare I even say that it's a *prime* time to discover to an even greater degree who we really are and all that we can be? As unique individuals, we have new paths to tread with many new freedoms that come at this stage. For instance, now we can think about things we never may have thought about before, such as letting go of the expectations of others, releasing obligations to which we can now say *no*, and embracing new opportunities to which we can now say *yes*.

The huge paradigm shift that happens in this new season brings a sweeping sense of liberation that replaces our former constraints and pressures. We become unchained in our hearts and are free to discover the world in a fresh, new way.

Allow me to give a brief tour to your imagination of some simple pleasures and possibilities on your new horizon. Have you ever thought about enjoying things that are aesthetically preferable to your taste that you may not have indulged in before transition because you felt restrained for some reason? Perhaps there are colors and decorations you want to put on your walls just because you like them. Maybe there are styles and fashions you want to wear simply because they fit your personality. Maybe you'd like to take a class that intrigues you. Why not buy specialty food items to keep in your fridge—foods that go beyond necessities, but that you love for the sheer enjoyment of them? You may have time to take fitness classes now. You finally can see those movies you've always wanted to see. And there's so much more—stories to tell, books to read, journals to write, perfumes to buy, new songs to sing—the list goes on.

It's your time! Yes, it's *your* time—like a blank canvas just waiting for your creative brushstrokes and as unique as your own fingerprint. You are free to be *you*! This truly is a time of adventure, introspection, and exploration.

One of my own small discoveries was that I could listen to music that was enjoyable to me. I spent so many years giving other people's music preferences priority. After the transition of my children growing up and moving out, I remember my son-in-law asking me, "Mom, what kind of music do you like?" As I rattled off songs I had heard via the kids or at church, he stopped me and said, "Mom, what kind of music do *you* enjoy personally?" Wow. I never had really given it any thought. I had been going with the flow for so long that I had lost my individuality in this area. The more I thought about what sounds I liked, the more I realized how much I love specific music—soft jazz and cello instrumentals. What about you? What kind of music do you like?

Maybe you long to go on a retreat or to take a getaway. If you could go anywhere, where would it be? There's so much beauty to explore. The planet is a big, beautiful world that God has created. I've always wanted to take a train ride through the Midwest. Specialty trains have sleeping cars and stop at various exciting destinations. This may not be your cup of tea, but that's okay, because I'm discovering my own cup of tea. There are old friendships to invest more time into and new friendships to make. There are more kisses and hugs to give your grandchildren, who see you as the loveliest superhero of all—even this is evidence of this very special time of life.

Maybe you never thought about it in this way. Maybe you thought you were destined to wither from this point on, spending your time thinking about days gone by and how things used to be before they changed. That's what everyone thought about the old house my husband and I bought—that it had seen its best days. So many passersby shook their heads in despair. But after we bought it, our neighbors, who had been in the neighborhood for fifty years, came over and thanked us. When the yearlong renovations were complete, they remarked that the house never had looked so good.

Listen—if God were done with you on this earth, you would not be here. You are here for a reason and for His purposes. Many times in Scripture, God used people in special ways during their mature years, including Sarah, Abraham, Moses, Anna, Elizabeth, Noah, and Enoch. Years seasoned with life experience are a unique time to explore who you are in Christ and to contemplate why you believe the things you believe. Maybe you need to make changes even in this area. It may be time to reevaluate your commitments and allegiances. Perhaps redirection is in order. Aligning yourself with the saints of old to a greater degree while you are still on this earth brings a sense of the divine to the ground. Truly, there is no greater adventure than being an integral part of this great cloud of witnesses.

No one knows better than those who reach the mature years that life is short. We know this more keenly because we have seen how fast the years have already flown. We have a certain designated amount of time left here on earth. What will it look like? This sober reality plays a part in the vision for our future, making it purposeful. The psalmist expresses this sentiment in Psalm 90:12 for this very reason: "Teach us to number our days," he says, "that we may gain a heart of wisdom." He desired to live out the rest of his days with a deeper understanding in the richest sense possible of the wisdom that comes from awareness of the brevity of life.

When we venture down our unique path, we find it strewn with the sweetest of rose petals ushering us forward. Each petal represents a word of truth softly placed under our feet by the Spirit, who cares deeply for our souls. There is rest from old perspectives and revival from new ones.

Just thinking about the possibilities feels refreshing, doesn't it? And this hope is possible when we walk with the Lord. Consider the following passage of Scripture and notice the striking relevance: "The LORD is my Shepherd.... He makes me lie down in green pastures. He leads me beside still waters. He restores my soul. He leads me in paths of righteousness" (Psalm 23:1–3 ESV). Oh, how our hearts need this!

As you read this book, my prayer is that you will catch the vision of all you can be in this period of exceptional blooming of your life. There is so much possibility to thrill your soul and motivate your heart like never before. There is more to this time than merely the fact that it is a new season of life. It offers a unique blend of freedom and maturation.

Its dimensions will be wider because you are wiser; its fragrance will be sweeter as your dependence on God deepens; its color will become increasingly vivid as you access God's built-in provision—just as He provided for the bromeliad in my backyard for so many years even when no one took notice. This period in your life is a choice time to bloom. It offers an exceptional and exciting adventure of discovering a new identity that belongs only to you.

EXCEPTIONAL BLOOM

There is more to the bromeliad than meets the eye. It has an unconventional strength. Even when other plants wither, the bromeliad blossoms vibrantly. This is because its growth is not dependent on its circumstances. Indeed, there is an exceptional design in this plant, and each individual plant has its own history. Regardless of that history, the stunning bromeliad is free to bloom.

2

Divine Evaluation

After casting the vision and considering potential possibilities, the next step is to bring it before the Lord in prayerful and thoughtful evaluation. Our goal here is to shift *our* idea of what's next to *His* idea of what's next. This becomes an intentional aligning of our vision with God's desire for our future. As we do this, we will notice a pink hue begin to form on the distant horizon, offering hope, new direction, and beauty.

The word *beauty* brings to mind different things for different people. Some think of hairstyles, others think of fashion, and yet others, a good diet and exercise plan. Marketers and advertisers often promote beauty "secrets" simply because the word *secret* sells. According to Oberlo Statistics, in 2023, the global beauty industry is expected to make $571 billion.

What if I told you there really is a secret to *true* beauty—the kind of beauty that matters? We will discover that secret in this chapter.

But first, I'd better start from the beginning. I have to be honest and tell you that when we decided to buy the old house, I wouldn't let anyone know where it was located until its initial renovations were complete. The place was unlivable, so we stayed in a condo while it was being worked on. For some reason, I felt the need to shelter my angst and uncertainty of the process from inquisitive eyes. What was driving the need for protection? I wrestled with this question and eventually realized it was because of the stage of transition the house (as well as my heart) was in. We were in the "evaluation" phase, and this took time, contemplation, and soul searching. Moving from a large home brimming with young family life and then buying this broken-down home that no longer would hold these activities begged the question: What would it all look like? What was God's plan (not just our plan) for our next season and for this old house? The truth is, moving from one season to another is a passage that is not always easy. In fact, sometimes it's just plain hard.

Earlier, we discovered that my husband had cancer. It was a very traumatic period for us—a time of surgery, treatment, and unsure results. If you've experienced anything similar, you understand how much a crisis of this magnitude can shake your world. We became solemnly aware of just how fragile life is. It was also at this time that our eyes were opened in a humble way to the grandness of God.

I'll never forget how the doctor pulled me aside after my husband's surgery and said, "If only he had come to me eight months earlier." My husband had two malignant tumors removed from his bladder. The surgeon's trained eye saw an aggressive cancer that had been growing for too long and had entered the wall lining. There was concern it had passed through and metastasized. It was obvious, without the doctor saying so directly, that he thought it was too late. I felt so helpless and quickly found myself overwhelmed with visible grief.

The women's-ministry director from our local church heard about my husband's surgery and came to the hospital on her own initiative. She was waiting for me in the lobby. When she saw me enter the room with tear-filled eyes, she rushed to give me a firm embrace and urged me to try to stop crying and be strong. To her it was an "ugly" scene to have a Christian weeping. But here's the thing—God doesn't see it that way. My tears mattered to Him, and they needed *shelter*, *protection*, and *space* for safe processing. So, after thanking her for coming, I swiftly ushered her out the door so I could be myself—tears and all—before God.

Likewise, the old house, with all that would be torn down to be rebuilt, needed time and space for the changes that needed to take place. Intrusions, judgments, or expectations from outside influences might complicate the process and not be beneficial.

It was during this dark season of cancer that God led me to a verse that became one of reverence and wonder to my soul: "This far you may come and no farther; here is where your proud waves halt" (Job 38:11).

Upon reading this truth about God's staggering authority, a sense of *fear and wonder* came over me, and I became acutely aware that He was in total control. If He had boundaries for the movement of the waves in the ocean, He could have boundaries for the cancer, too. Now, that didn't mean He wouldn't take my husband home if He chose to do so, but rather, that the future was ultimately in His hands. This verse whispered truth of an otherworldly nature deep into my soul. I was struck with awe at the thought of God's supremacy! My husband's and my lives belonged to Him. With fear and trembling knees and a tear-stained face, I placed my trust in the outcome to God—whatever it was to be. If He was calling us to face death, He would walk with us through it. You can imagine my surprise—and the doctor's complete shock—to find out a few days later this aggressive cancer had not spread. He even noted that it was nothing less than a miracle.

The Lord did a sobering work in our hearts that season, setting a whirlwind of change in motion. It was spiritual and pivotal, and it was centered on the greatest beautifying source of all—the fear of the Lord.

There you have it—the most extreme and exquisite beauty treatment of all time. The Scriptures verify its value: "Charm is deceptive, and beauty is fleeting; but a woman who fears the LORD is to be praised" (Proverbs 31:30).

Maybe you are facing tremendous pain because your life is changing in ways you never could have foreseen. Your heart may be crying out, *Why, God?* Loss and change can be devastating. And—in case no one told you—it's okay to cry. Tears are beautiful to God (see Psalm 56:8). In fact, God desires to use your tears to bring you beyond the *why* to a richer country—the beautiful lands of a Job-like trust. Youth, strength, and self-confidence can keep us far from its border, but the pain of losing *a time of life* so very dear to us can become the catalyst that is to this higher ground. The world might rude awakening, but for the Christian, it is divine awakening.

Do you remember what God said to Job when Job asked the Lord for the meaning of his suffering? In Job 38:4, God said, "Where were you when I laid the earth's foundation?" In other words, God was letting Job know that it wasn't about getting the answers to life but trusting that the Author of life had the answers. God went on to blow Job's mind even further by asking him questions that continued to reveal God's unfathomable ability to hold *all* of life's answers and keep everything into perspective. Here are some of the questions God put to Job:

Have you ever given orders to the morning, or shown the dawn its place? (Job 38:12)

Have you journeyed to the springs of the sea or walked in the recesses of the deep? (Job 38:16)

Have you entered the storehouses of the snow or seen the storehouses of the hail? (Job 38:22)

Do you send the lightning bolts on their way? Do they report to you, "Here we are"? (Job 38:35)

Job's response after having his own eyes opened to an awareness of God's majesty and total control was no longer "Why?" but essentially "Why not?" Job humbly and fearfully replied, "I know that You can do all things; no purpose of Yours can be thwarted" (Job 42:2). In its newfound fear of the Lord, Job's heart began to expand in a marvelous way as never before.

The Bible tells us that the fear of the Lord is the beginning of wisdom, knowledge, and understanding (see Proverbs 9:10). This expansion is part of our spiritual blooming. In fact, the wisdom that comes from *the fear of the Lord* is the cornerstone, key, and starting place in the cultivation process of the beauty of this exceptional bloom—whether it's the old house that had further potential than its original standing, or you, who have further potential than your original identity. From God's perspective, there is so much more for you than you ever may have recognized or realized. Taking a fresh look in awe and reverence from His holy ground shapes your blossoming.

It's amazing to consider—while many people spend years in vain chasing a fountain of youth that doesn't exist, we have received direct access to the most transforming fountain of all time. Proverbs 14:27 (ESV) tells us, "The fear of the LORD is a fountain of life." We are free to drink deeply from the waters of this fountain, and doing so creates an inward beauty that is exquisite and refreshing beyond compare.

Think about it for a moment. Don't we all know women who radiate beauty from the inside? They may be older and not as physically attractive as they once were, but their hearts are so attractive that somehow their outer beauty is affected. Their eyes sparkle, and their smiles shine. There is something in these women that is free from the expectations of others and is deeply rooted in Christ. Such women are like a fountain that overflows with communion and fellowship with the divine. They are like Moses when he came down from the mountain after having spent intimate time with the Lord. His face glowed with God's presence. Can you think of anything more beautiful?

So it was with the old house. Even though we had caught the vision of what it could be, we spent a sober time in evaluation before the Lord of what it *needed to be*. What intentions might the Lord have for this home? How did He see it? What could we change about it to give it an even greater purpose? What could we keep the same but use in smarter ways? We considered and evaluated all of these things. It was no longer about keeping up with others' expectations (or our own) because something greater and more substantial was in store.

I couldn't help but be reminded of the old and stinky barn that held baby Jesus—so rough, crude, and unimpressive. Yet, how precious that place was.

Why?

Because it was used for God's sacred purpose. It became so beautiful in sentiment to His beloved people that the memory of this humble abode is celebrated yearly at Christmas with manger scenes displayed on lawns, in churches, and in storefronts all across the world. Just catching a glimpse of one fills us with otherworldly warmth. This is what the fear of the Lord does in our hearts. It takes what we might normally consider *not so valuable* and makes it *very valuable*. And likewise, it takes what we might consider very valuable and makes it not so valuable. For instance, one would naturally think a king would be born in a fancy palace, but God was pleased to have His Son born in an unremarkable manger. Therefore, a palace—no matter how impressive—pales in comparison to this barn scene. The greater our fear of the Lord, the more we will want to align with His value system and see it as beautiful.

The phrase *fear of the Lord* is often misunderstood. Some think it is a fear-based feeling that makes us anxious to meet some standard of perfection. This is not what the Bible refers to when it speaks of the fear of the Lord. Our own perfection is never the goal, but rather, trusting God in the difficulties and brokenness and when things don't make sense. *Strong's Dictionary* describes *fear* in this context as "reverence." It's recognizing as Job did that God's ways are beyond ours. In other words, it is an inner awe and uncommon wonder caused by an intensified awareness of the bigness of God.

Let me try to convey this concept in earthly terms. Many years ago, when we were hosting a casual gathering at our home, my daughter, who was seventeen at the time, handed me a paper cup and a pen and asked me to write my name on the cup. Quite puzzled because she had written everyone else's names on their cups, I asked her why she hadn't written mine on my cup. Her answer astonished me. She said she felt uncomfortable casually writing out my first name because of the honor she felt for me as her mother. I couldn't help marveling as I considered such *uncommon* reverence.

Let me contrast this to a time when I was serving in a Sunday-school class for three-year-olds. A little boy was hitting some of the other children, so I gently knelt down and lovingly but firmly told him not to hit the other kids. Right then and there, he drew his hand back, and as hard as he could, he slapped me across the face. I was stunned. I couldn't scold him, as he wasn't my child, but I was in shock. I just stood up and walked away quietly. This kind of tender direction always had worked with my kids, but they had a healthy respect for and honoring of me. And there is the difference. I was not very big to the little boy, and because of that, he did not respect me. However, in my children's hearts, I was very big, which was reflected in their deep love and devotion to me and ultimately the choices they made when they were young.

How big God is to us in this unique season of our lives will be reflected in our love, honor, and devotion to Him. Cultivating an *uncommon* reverence is dazzling!

In the first chapter of this book, I touched on the brevity of life, a realization of which fosters a healthy fear of the Lord. This is one of the most beautiful parts of the season of exceptional bloom: instead of looking at our earthly life as endless and all about us, we start to see our lives as temporal and a part of His bigger plan. There are things in this plan that we may not have recognized or even realized and that need fresh evaluation.

Sometimes we miss this opportunity because we feel stuck. We are sad because certain things have passed us by. Many times, we placed our value and formed our identity in those things. Some of those things we worked hard for, and some were obligations placed on us by others. Regardless, they seem different now—they're either fading or gone completely from our lives, and we feel as though their absence diminishes our value. Maybe things didn't turn out as we had planned, and we feel disappointed and disenchanted. And if we are grieving the loss of a central part of our lives, the pain of loss can be crippling. Yet, the more we recognize that God works even *great loss* into His bigger plan, the more we can trust Him to walk us through the pain—He knew loss too. The transition stage of life is the perfect time to cultivate our purpose and value in Christ and see it as a season sovereignly designed by God to do so.

Your identity is not gradually diminishing at this time of life as the world would have you think. This period is only the beginning of finding out who you are in Christ, and fearing the Lord is the threshold. There is so much to explore and learn from here. "The fear of the LORD is the beginning..." (Proverbs 1:7 ESV).

Placing your vision in humble submission before the throne of God is the divine starting line. You previously may have been this or that, but now you are on a mission to discover who you are in this new season. The answers are not centered on how you previously saw yourself or how others saw you but on how God sees you now. He'll use plenty of structures from the past, but He'll make new structures and demolish some old ones as well. Remember, some things will be just plain hard, but others will be exciting adventures.

Let me ask you some basic and brief questions to get your thinking process flowing. Take all these thoughts to the Lord in prayer. Write down or tuck away in your heart what the Lord shows you. And please give yourself the freedom and room to explore and laugh—and by all means, cry when needed.

OLD STRUCTURES

What is important in your life that you believe God would have you continue to invest in? Is it your children, grandchildren, husband, extended family, neighbors, friends, or ministries? Often, it isn't until the season of exceptional bloom that these parts of our lives become recognizably valuable to us. I remember seeing an interview with Billy Graham once. I was struck by his answer to the question of what he would have done differently if he could go back in time. He openly shared that he would have spent more time with his family, and he admitted that he hadn't realized this until his later season of life. This type of awareness initially might spark a sentiment of sadness in your heart of having missed opportunities, but it's a blessing in disguise. This awareness is a compass God can use to redirect your priorities for the future. This is exactly what Billy Graham set out to do in his new season, with the Lord's leading. You can be sure that family time in the Graham clan took on a richer depth.

NEW STRUCTURES

What are some new things you would like to invest your time in that you have not done? For instance, God may have designed you with unique gifts and interests specific to you that you never have really tapped into. Maybe it's reading, art, going back to school, traveling, dancing, studying nutrition, or exercising. These ideas can feel either exciting or intimidating because they are new prospects. Plus, now you must readjust your thinking to accept that you are free to do these activities. In other words, you previously may have said no to this or that, but now you can say *yes*!

Also, there may be studies that you might like to engage in to better understand certain issues in your life. This is a great time to reevaluate why you think the way you do. You can even take constructive and beneficial classes or get counseling to help focus on these areas and heal them if need be.

STRUCTURES OUT OF SEASON

Are there some things you may have placed too much value on that you are realizing are not as important as you thought once you set them before the Lord? Maybe there are habitual structures that were part of your past but don't fit into your future. Perhaps you need to break from relationships or activities that have become unhealthy.

What about those seasons of great value in your life that have come to an end? If they had a meaningful hold on your heart, then moving forward may seem impossible. This loss can be the most difficult to consider because the pain is most grievous. Treasuring a valuable season from the past while simultaneously discovering a new sense of identity in the present can feel very incompatible. Naturally so. In the next chapter, we will look in-depth at why it may feel impossible as well as explore needed tools to work through this process. Remember, the same God who gave you the gift of your previous season is caring for you now and will make a way for your future. Priming your heart toward reverence in His ability to develop in you a Job-like trust is where you start. Your new season has been on His divine calendar since the beginning. Keep in mind, Job needed time and space to grieve great loss. God even rebuked Job's well-meaning friends for interfering in the process. He described their "help" as darkening counsel with words without knowledge (see Job 38:2)—hence the wisdom of sheltering yourself during the angst and uncertainty of transition. Yet, as uncertain as it may feel on your end, God has it completely under control. All these losses are a part of expanding your heart for the exceptional bloom He has planned just for you.

For my husband and me, God used cancer to reveal the importance of breaking from a false confidence that everything stays the same. He also used my empty nest as a way for me to bloom as an individual, not just as a mother. He used the deaths of my parents and dear friends to draw me nearer to the reality of heaven. Although these events were losses, they all were a part of the shaping process of the season in life that is unique and full of new opportunities that lovingly treasure the old while embracing the new.

Remember that God is doing something new and beautiful in you. Taking the vision in the first chapter and bringing it before the fear of Lord only makes it lovelier.

But there is more to consider. Join me in diving

even deeper into this special, once-in-a-lifetime season. A magnificent bloom awaits you.

EXCEPTIONAL BLOOM

That beloved old bromeliad! Even if it thought it was in trouble from changing and turbulent conditions, God reminded it that He indeed had a plan all along. Not only for its survival but also for its exceptional bloom—for God's ways are wondrously big!

3

The Preparation Process

y now, you may see a few bright glimmers of pink finally breaking through your once-perpetually grey-toned sky. Be assured these rays will be coming in greater measure. But first, there are a few storm clouds to work through. After you have cast the vision of what could be and soberly evaluated your situation from the foundation of having a reverent fear of the Lord, it's time to consider the preparation.

When I was in my twenties, I was quite the rebel. In fact, trouble seemed to follow me wherever I went—until I had four beautiful daughters, all born within four years. My gratitude to God for these precious girls moved me like nothing ever had moved me before. I always had known about God, but it never made a difference in the way I chose to live—until then.

Looking back, I realize that I was largely driven by failed expectations of myself. I was the stereotypical black sheep of the family, but when my daughters arrived, all that changed. I was determined to raise them differently and give them as wholly as I could to the Lord. It was a rich time for me spiritually, even though I became a single mother. Raising my children created an almost magical season in my life, and I felt God's favor greatly. After a few years, the Lord even brought a new husband into the picture. He was the girls' Sunday-school teacher, which made it an even dreamier scenario. He became a father to them, and they got a brand-new baby sister soon thereafter. Could it get any better?

Fast-forward to a new season of my life, one in which my four older daughters were all grown up. Three had married, and the last of the four I had just dropped off at Moody Bible Institute in Chicago. I was on my way back to the airport to fly home when a crazy deluge of feelings came over me. *What if God's favor is removed from my life now that all my older girls are gone? What if I turn back into the one who always expects to fail?* Being struck with fear, the questions kept coming. *Is the bottom falling out from beneath a wonderful season, and is the proverbial clock about to strike midnight?* I felt as though my once-unshakable confidence was being ripped from my hands. Frantic thoughts engulfed me as I considered the unknown.

Sure enough, when I got to the airport, little things started to unravel. The taxi driver dropped me off at the wrong terminal. I had to trudge through wet snow to get to the right one, which meant I completely soaked my already iced-over toes. When I made it inside to the airport-security line, the alarm went off as I walked through the scanner. They gave me a pat down, which felt invasive. When I finally made my way to my seat, I found myself squashed against the window by two large men who were so tall that their knees pressed tightly against the backs of the seats in front of them, blocking me in. There was no getting out. I didn't even have enough room to shift in my seat or bend down to remove my icy shoes. So, there I sat, wedged in with bitter-cold boots, wondering if this was the beginning of a season of decline.

I felt overwhelmed and started to weep. The flight attendant came over and handed me tissues, probably thinking I was grieving and on a flight back from a funeral. And you know what? I really was grieving. There might as well have been a funeral because I was experiencing the profound sense of loss of the way things were. Fear of the future only intensified this reality. In the transition my life was facing, not only did I need time and space to work through the emotions of grief—I needed basic means and provisions. Understanding the mechanics of the grieving process provided these much-needed tools to work through fear of the unknown. All of this was a part of the preparation process God had planned for this season of my life. Although an exceptional bloom certainly was in store for me, in order to get there, I would need to engage these tools to work through serious prep time.

Prepping for anything can be difficult. Getting a renovation project up and running often requires quite a bit of groundwork. For us women who are facing advancing years, it's no different. To a certain degree, we all share a common necessity for preparation as we begin this unique season in our lives. Wrapping our minds around this concept not only connects us—it brings a sense of clarity during an unsettling time.

In terms of the house we were renovating, laying the groundwork meant being prepared for the messy unpredictability of the work involved. Before we proceeded, the contractor cautioned us that the house would look significantly worse before it looked better—and did it ever! There was bulldozing, sanding, blasting, cutting, gutting, and several other adjustments before the work was

complete. He told us the house inevitably w
in shambles, with glass and rubble everywhere. ...
so, we were not alarmed, because we understood
that this was a normal aspect of the renovation
process.

As you can imagine, whenever we took a walk
through the house while it was in this condition
so that we could inspect the work in progress, we
experienced conflicting feelings. On the one hand,
we could envision glimmers of what it would look
like—cabinets here or there, beautiful granite
counters, a lovely tiled bath. On the other hand, the
house was looking even further removed from that
picture in our minds than when we started, as if the
process were going in the wrong direction. Merely
peeling back the old carpet revealed damage we had
not anticipated having to repair. The renovation
became a bigger project than we had thought.

The same holds true for us. There is an unset-
tledness and unpredictability as we move through
a season of change. During this stage, we may even
need to take a sabbatical from some of our typical
activities—not because there's anything wrong with
them, but because our feelings can be volatile while
getting ready for what's next. As our hearts undergo
the natural process of preparation, they may even
look like the construction site of our house—only

with confusion and emotions rather than glass and rubble. We may even discover that our period of transition has turned out to be a bigger project than we expected.

If this describes how you are feeling in any way, know that you are not alone. This is a very normal experience in transition. And if you are in the season of advancing years, you think you should have it all together, but that's the pressure society puts on you—especially in church. You actually can't have it all together because each transition is new, with unique variables to the person experiencing it.

You need to know that in the preparation stage, feelings of grief are very normal, as I described in the story about my flight home from Chicago. Most people don't make the correlation between grief and transition. But understanding that there is loss associated with change helps you process and make sense of the confusing and often messy emotions involved. For this reason, familiarizing yourself with the stages of grief is important.

There are five universal stages of grief: denial, anger, bargaining, depression, and acceptance. As you consider these stages in your season of transition, you may recognize yourself at any point. Simply making the connection helps in the processing, providing a mental map to navigate the unknown.

Reflect on some of the changes you have gone through or are personally facing. Sometimes people face multiple changes at once. Are you staring at an empty nest and unsure of your role in life now that your children are grown? Maybe you are facing estrangement from a family member. Are you going through divorce? Have you needed to make a career change and thought you would never have to face that at this stage in life? Are you dealing with physical challenges? Maybe you're struggling with health issues, and it is difficult to remain hopeful about the future. You may have experienced the death of a friend or loved one, and it threw you off balance because it brought the reality of aging and death closer to the forefront.

If you have experienced any of these life-altering events, your first response may have been denial. This is quite common, as denial is the first stage of the grieving process one experiences when facing major life change. Denial actually helps you survive the loss you are facing. Because loss is so overwhelming, you feel "at a loss" (dazed) as well. This is denial kicking in and acting as a protection mechanism. It helps you to pace your feelings of grief, and it cushions the intense impact of what you are going through. You're not denying the truth of the loss, but rather, your mind dials down the loss to anesthetize you against the pain.

This is where I found myself after the last of my older daughters left home. Honestly, there aren't many books written on this subject, especially for Christians. So, I did what any well-meaning Christian would do in a time like this: I threw myself into ministry. It's what I knew best, and it became my mode of denial. It helped numb the pain. The doors swung wide open for me, too. Please don't misunderstand—I don't think there's anything wrong with being more involved in ministry in this time of life. It may even be helpful. But to deny our feelings or hide them in ministry because we don't like the discombobulated way we feel will only prolong the inevitable. Remember, in the grieving process, denial is a temporary cushion to help us reach the next stage of the journey we must face.

This brings us to the second stage, which is anger. Anger is a very normal response to change as our feelings begin to intensify, coming more into focus. During this time, we are prone to make sarcastic remarks about how our lives have shifted. Anger actually gives us a sense of structure after feeling lost and disconnected for so long. We may not like the feeling, but anger is a good sign that we are emerging from denial. I'm not talking about destructive anger, but a normal and healthy anger that surfaces with grief. This kind of anger is often exhibited in feelings of frustration with a current loss. Before we worry that this isn't Biblical, we can be assured that Scripture states that anger is not only normal but also good. Ecclesiastes 7:3 tells us, "Frustration is better than laughter, because a sad face is good for the heart."

My husband used to get angry and joke that our daughters were stolen away by our sons-in-law. I laughed to myself because I knew he really didn't mean those words literally—he was simply processing how his heart felt. It was a sign that he was coming out of the coma-like state of denial I saw him go into after the girls were married.

Since anger can be an emotionally heightened stage of the grieving process, we must be cautious of bridges we might be inclined to burn. At this juncture, we are more likely to say things that hurt others, so we must guard our words with care. Yet we should not stuff or stifle our feelings either but work through them instead. Taking time to process our anger and hurt feelings with a trusted friend can be very helpful. Confiding in someone who doesn't condemn us but also is careful not to fuel the anger is beneficial. It's important to identify those people who are "safe" so they can walk through the process of transition with us. A sound support system during transition is invaluable.

The third stage in the grieving process is bargaining. We bargain with God to return life to some sort of familiarity—how life used to be. We go back to the past and dwell on the way things were. We ruminate on ways we can perhaps salvage the loss. Our minds come up with hundreds of scenarios to make it better.

We often don't realize we are bargaining. Sometimes when we suffer loss on one end, we try to make up for it on the other. We seek out connections to the loss and pursue them. For example, in a failed relationship, even though the person is gone, the hurt party may look for similar traits of that person in other people. For instance, if a woman's ex-boyfriend possesses a certain characteristic she misses, she may look for that same dynamic in another man to stay in the realm of familiarity. This is certainly understandable, especially if it's a good trait, but she might miss out on recognizing an amazing person with different qualities that could potentially be a better fit for her.

Once we begin to surface from denial, anger, and bargaining, we might find ourselves smack dab in the middle of the fourth stage, which is depression. At this point, we start to realize that those things that once defined our identity have changed for good and are not coming back. We begin to question our value and our future. This also is normal, but life can feel insurmountable at this juncture. The good news is that this is the final stage of grief before acceptance. Once we experience depression, we are almost through the grieving process and ready to flourish. But there is no skipping this step—we must go through it.

Sometimes, transition coincides with a woman's greatest biological and hormonal changes. We must factor this in, because it inevitably will have an effect on the way we feel. Declining estrogen levels can cause increased irritability, sadness, anxiety, fatigue, mood swings, and tension, as well as a lack of motivation. Recognizing this will help us understand why we may be having a harder time than usual dealing with the changes around us. (Notice that I did not use the "m" word, as promised in the beginning of this book!)

Just like the old house, we might need to take some time to be off-limits as we regroup and go through this very natural process of reorienting. After much prayer, I decided to do just that. I let my pastor know that I would be stepping away from ministry for a season. Many people didn't see me in the church halls and wondered whether I was okay, but what I was experiencing was very normal. I didn't need to worry if people didn't understand, nor did I feel obliged to explain. How do you explain something you haven't figured out yourself? This period of stepping back was very freeing for me.

During this time, some major changes happened. At certain moments, it seemed as though getting through it all was an impossible challenge, and like the old house, there was complete breakdown. Yet even this was a part of the beautifying process of what God had in store for me in the exceptional blooming of what was to come next. As discouraging as this time felt, it was of enormous value while God prepared me by shaking things up—a winnowing of sorts—loosening my grip, and getting me ready for a season characterized by a deeper color and a more fragrant bloom.

We see this process at work in First Peter 5:10 (NKJV), which states, "May the God of all grace, who called us to His eternal glory by Christ Jesus, after you have suffered a while, perfect, establish, strengthen, and settle you." The last four verbs of this verse—*perfect, establish, strengthen,* and *settle*—give us significant insight into our preparation for the exceptional-blooming season that God has planned for us.

In this verse, the verb *perfect* in *Strong's Dictionary*

is described as "adjust." It gives the sense of arranging or putting a thing in its appropriate position. We can see how this works marvelously in this season of grieving and suffering as it allows our hearts to be spiritually repositioned in the amazing direction of discovering who we really are in Christ. As we come closer to the reality of our ultimate heavenly destination, God sets our hearts in order and positions us in a very intimate connection with Him. We begin to grasp that life is short and uncertain and sense our need for greater dependence on and connectedness to God's larger design.

The word *establish* in *Strong's Dictionary* means "to turn resolutely in a certain direction." We can see again how wonderfully the process continues, as the Lord not only spiritually rearranges our hearts but also causes us to turn from our old way of living and resolve to move forward in a new direction. God divinely coaxes us out of the empty nest or previous season of life as well as unrealized ideas of how we think life should have turned out. Why should we stay there and bemoan all that was when a new world has opened up to us? With our spiritual senses, we begin to experience a very strong reality of this otherworldliness.

Thayer's Greek Lexicon describes the word *strengthen* as "to make strong." In other words, where there once were spiritual weakness, infirmity, and disease, now there is spiritual strength. What we were once so certain about we discover is not so certain. Life is always changing. Giving up our own reasonings and logic allows us to be strengthened in trusting God. We again can see how perfectly this process unfolds. God rearranges our hearts spiritually; then He encourages us to follow this spiritual realignment resolutely; and finally, He strengthens us to take the necessary steps to go through the process. The Holy Spirit gently guides and helps us every step of the way. Here we are on a road we never thought we'd survive, let alone travel, but we are doing both and thriving as God opens our eyes to new and deep treasures that come only in this season.

The last word in our list, *settle*, *Thayer's Greek Lexicon* describes as "to lay a foundation," meaning that a ground has been readied (noted in the three previous verbs) for building to commence. We see now that as suffering has its perfect work in our lives—bringing us through a rearranging of the heart, to following resolutely in that direction, and to being strengthened and brought to spiritual wellness—we are settled and grounded in the fear of the Lord and ready for a new work to be built on this refined foundation. There is certainly a thrill and excitement in considering all that lies ahead and contemplating what it will look like.

With all this said, you might recognize yourself somewhere in the middle of the preparation stage—the place of being sure and unsure about your future and what you want to accomplish. Maybe you are hiding behind a title or a position. Perhaps, in order to numb some of the emotions, you are getting involved in projects or activities that aren't really you. Maybe you are stuck and feel immobilized. You might be facing deep regret or depression. Don't let any of this throw you. Recognize that you are being readied for a great work.

With the Lord's help, let your heart continue through the process. He has wonderful plans in store for you. This stage is simply a bridge so that you can cross over to the other side, where the final stage, which is acceptance, awaits you.

Acceptance is the beautiful place where we come to terms with the reality that what was once normal to us has changed, and there is a new normal to embrace. This new normal might bring on feelings of anticipation. We no longer feel obligated to the old season to the degree that we did when we were just beginning to grieve our life change. Instead, we have a fresh outlook and a looser hold on the past as we look to the future.

I must caution, however, that heavy spiritual warfare may present itself at this juncture. In the next chapter, we will discuss how to keep watch during the preparation period so that this stage powerfully and victoriously brings us to the most exceptional bloom we've ever known in our lives this side of heaven.

EXCEPTIONAL BLOOM

There is a period in the bromeliad's life cycle when there is no sign of bloom. Before it blossoms into something magnificent, the plant almost looks as though it is nearing the end. By all appearances, it should be plucked out of the ground and tossed aside. If that were to happen, though, the plant would never experience its most dynamic season—a blooming season that is categorically different from the growing seasons. What a shame and waste it would be to disregard its potential merely because it looks like it's past its prime. It hasn't even begun its exceptional bloom.

4

Keeping Watch

At this point, you may sense the promising hope of a fresh horizon. The subtle shades of soft pink in the previous chapters may have offered encouragement to your soul, but beware: at this juncture, Satan is most eager to cast an ugly spirit of darkness to thwart any forward movement. He knows God has great hope in store for you, and he doesn't want that forward movement to happen. This brings us to the fourth step in the blooming process. After casting the vision for your next season, soberly evaluating it from the foundation of the holy fear of the Lord, and undergoing preparations for stepping into that season, you will need to keep watch and remain alert to Satan's opportunistic ways of obstructing spiritual flourishing.

I distinctly remember when I was under great

spiritual oppression. It was during the season of preparation—a time of significant stress due to the natural process of grieving. As I tried to make sense of what was happening in my life, I decided to head to our waterfront fishing cabin on the west coast of Florida. A trip by myself to seek the Lord was just what I needed, so I packed my bags, loaded my big, clunky dog into the car, and headed out. When I arrived, the ocean channel was pristine as always. The water was glistening, and the fish were jumping. Soon after I settled in, a prancing dolphin greeted me as I sat in deep thought on the back-porch swing. While listening to the waves splashing against the sea wall, I was reminded of how much I love the tranquility of this quaint little cabin. I felt grateful to be at such a serene location to put my thoughts in order.

The next day, I awoke to a breathtaking morning. I grabbed my Bible and a cup of coffee and headed out to the deck. The ocean breezes were blowing softly, and again the sun was shining. I was sitting in the rocker when suddenly I was startled by my dog, who was barking and running toward the edge of the porch. When I looked up, I saw a troubling sight—hundreds of black vultures circling directly above. They began diving down and swooping in on my yapping companion. Overcome with fear, I grabbed my dog by the collar and pulled her inside. Shaken to the core, I heard the vultures' sharp claws scratching on my tin roof as they landed one by one. It was eerie, like a scene out of a horror movie. In tears, I called my husband. What did all of this mean? This had never happened before in all the times we'd come to the cabin together. Why now, when I was facing such loss? It was just so creepy.

The vultures circled in the sky and converged on my roof for hours. Feeling troubled in spirit, I prayed earnestly to the Lord for clarity.

Amazingly, God placed upon my heart a very distinct impression: I was in a season in which I faced the death of a life I once had known. This was why I was there—to grieve loss and to seek answers. The Lord graciously allowed a very real image for me to take hold of and never forget. In this picture, the vultures represented the spiritual darkness that converges on anything that smells of death. Often, we don't get to see such a vivid depiction of spiritual warfare, yet God was giving me this privilege. It became clear that Satan's agenda was to make me feel, think, and believe that my life was over. Certainly, a phase of my life had passed, so he was partially correct. Yet, in that same instance, God reminded me that I was not dead, as Satan would have me think. I was, indeed, still very much alive.

It was an epiphany of sorts—a spiritual parallel imprinted in my mind permanently. Maybe you haven't had an experience like this, but you have sensed spiritual oppression. We often don't see the clamoring that goes on in the heavens, yet the enemy seizes times in our lives like these to attack us when we are at our most vulnerable. Ephesians 6:12 talks about the spiritual warfare we face as Christians. The verse states, "Our struggle is not against flesh and blood, but against the rulers, against the authorities, against the powers of this dark world and against the spiritual forces of evil in the heavenly realms."

It was easy to see how this concept applied during the transition period of renovating our old house. We were unable to move in, which left the house vulnerable and exposed—it was an opportune time for mischief to occur. The place had a reputation for attracting squatters and transients. In its deepest decline, it was a crack house, as well as a place for dark practices of spiritism. Our neighbors informed us that the previous tenants had even placed signs on the street corner at nightfall that advertised psychic readings. The backyard was an ideal place for this type of enterprise, as it was private and surrounded by a mystical-looking rock garden.

In light of this reality, we decided to hire a

handyman to stay on the property (and sleep there) until we could move in. This way, the house would be safely guarded from people who used to frequent the house for drugs, and it would keep away any new troublemakers. When our appliances were installed, we were all the more grateful that someone was keeping an eye on our budding house.

Certainly, for us, when we are entering the next season of our lives, we are just as susceptible as my house was. This is a particularly "at-risk" period, when defenses are low. We can be sure that spiritual warfare will be fierce at this time. Satan is acutely aware of what gets us down, whether it's old regrets that haunt us or new fears that rush in. The more we understand which threats to keep watch for during the renovation process, the safer our journey to full bloom will be.

Keeping watch requires a keen awareness of our vulnerabilities, but we also must know what we are to look for in terms of Satan's tactics. Ironically, we don't have to look very far because his names reveal his intentions. He is Satan, the devil, the deceiver, the evil one—the enemy. Isn't it interesting that God would provide a clue in something as simple as a name so that we can take precautions? Can you imagine if it were that easy to evaluate a person's character in the present day? Although this isn't possible with humans, we do have insight into the schemes of our greatest spiritual enemy. As we examine some of Satan's names, consider how their meanings might manifest themselves in your season of change.

Strong's Dictionary describes the name "Satan" as "adversary" and "opponent." Satan will try to oppose the renovation process God has in mind for you by manipulating your emotions. He does this because emotions such as fear, doubt, insecurity, loneliness, bitterness, and feelings of inferiority are easy prey for him. He may even lunge on one in particular—the one you struggle with frequently. Like a lion on a hunt for the most accessible kill, Satan zeros in on that weak link so he can bring you down easily.

You shouldn't be surprised. This is what the adversary does—he opposes God, and he uses your own emotions to do it.

Notice that I didn't say that Satan opposes you personally. He would like nothing better than to win your affections (separate from God). If you take this season to pursue the priorities of the world rather than God's priorities, you are simply aligning yourself with Satan's temporal agenda. He is not going squash this. Satan is only out to oppose Jesus, who is in you.

Consider the three things noted in the Bible as Satan's definitive goals: to steal, kill, and destroy (see John 10:10). That is exactly what he is doing here. He is trying to extinguish your hope in what Christ is doing in your life by making you feel defeated. But note that only your *feelings* of defeat are being affected, because Satan has no real authority over you. This is crucial to remember.

Satan's strategy is to manipulate you with your own emotions.

Do you remember the scene in *The Wizard of Oz* when Toto pulled back the curtain to reveal that the big, intimidating wizard is really just an old man? All along, that old wizard was trying to conjure up an image in Dorothy's mind that his power was greater than it really was. Satan's smokescreen attempts to frighten you are similar to this. They're all about intimidation and trickery.

Let me pull back the curtain and show you that Satan isn't very powerful. He is just a created being and is no comparison to Christ, who is in you. Satan realizes he has lost the battle for your soul, so he instead spends his time continually trying to inflate your emotions with the goal of downsizing your hope.

Think about it. Maybe you've been experiencing heavy waves of discouragement as you realize that

a certain season has come to an end. Now add to
this a wave of fear—the fear of the future. On top
of this, add a wave of inferiority and another one
of uncertainty about your abilities. Can you see
the floodwaters mounting? These emotions can be
so overwhelming that they certainly do feel like a
black cloud of vultures converging upon you. Be
watchful, for though vultures circle, Christ—who
is in you—cannot be extinguished. The spiritual
person inside of you is very much alive!

Revelation 12:10 reminds us that Satan is "the
accuser" of the brothers and sisters. This brings
us to his second strategy revealed in the name
devil. Being an accuser means to falsely accuse,
slander, or defame in order to destroy. Have you
ever noticed how accusations divide people? We
see this in movies all the time. Someone accuses
a person, and immediately we see the division of
people and the formation of factions as the plot
thickens. In this season of your life, you may notice
that this phenomenon is occurring more frequently.
All sorts of issues seem to be divisive in nature.
The support you once had may now feel patchy at
best. Maybe you are being misunderstood by others
more than at any other time in your life. Perhaps
even your children are looking at you differently
and with a critical eye now that they are grown

or have spouses and children of their own. In this deliberate process, the devil is trying to break down your sense of community—the community and fellowship you have with friends and family and Christ. The devil wants others to see you in a defamatory way and vice versa. He knows the result will be breakdown and ultimate collapse of communication, relationships, and support. In fact, the devil will work overtime to try to destroy your connections in order to isolate you, and you may find yourself feeling very alone during this season of life.

In light of this strategy, taking steps to find the right kind of support is crucial. Establishing a safe support system with people who exhibit a genuine tone of warmth and interest in your spiritual well-being will help you tremendously in keeping watch. Allow this supportive circle to create a natural loving boundary around you.

It is also important to recognize that along with protecting your heart from other people's slander is the need to filter your own voice from Satan's attempts to make you your own worst accuser and critic. He may dredge up things from the past to remind you how you could have done this or that differently but how since you didn't, you are obviously a failure. He may come at you with that old lie that you never have been good enough, which makes you question why you would succeed now. If ever there was a time in life when the winds of inferiority blow, it is during the transition season headed toward the exceptional bloom.

So, be watchful. When you see the dark vultures of criticism swirling overhead, dive-bombing your confidence, remember that this is exactly the devil's strategy. He is trying to destroy you, but you will not be destroyed. You are and will remain very much alive, with the hope that God will stand with you and give you every ability and strength to succeed. As Philippians 4:13 reminds you, "I can do all this through Him who gives me strength."

The devil is also called "the deceiver," as he is the father of lies. All of his strategies are based on deception. If he can't squash your hope, he will try to transfer your hope to something faulty or empty. He does this by stirring aspirations in you to take the place of the hope you find in Christ. This is a replacement strategy. If he can get you to find hope in something other than Christ, he will have succeeded in his objective.

Let me give you a benign yet very telling example. The Christian world celebrates Christmas as a sacred holiday that marks when Christ was born. He is the reason for our hope at this season because

He is the greatest gift of all. But often, Santa, the biggest imaginary gift giver of all, replaces Jesus. Santa is not real, yet millions of children put their hopes in him; billions of dollars are made from merchandising him; countless movies, songs, and stories are created about him—and he doesn't even exist. Santa is a happy illusion—a replacement for real attention, focus, and hope.

In a season of transition, replacements can come in the form of material, physical, and superficial distractions. Allurements can grab hold of our hearts—such desirable seductions as body enhancements, new love interests, etc. Although we may entertain these enticements momentarily, we must soberly consider what we may be giving up in order to procure them. It's not so much that these things in themselves are all bad—and some may be harmless. But remember that replacement has the capacity to steal our affections from what really matters. All that glitters is not always gold. But there is treasure available to us in Christ that really is golden, and we have yet to embrace its gravity. (We will discuss this in depth in the next chapter.) In fact, in transition seasons, we are on the cusp of diving deeper into this richness in a more fulfilling way. Meanwhile, we should be aware that the devil will try to keep us from this sacred goldmine by deceiving us into believing that the grass is greener on the other side. Listen—it may be alluring, but the truth is that the strategy of replacement provides only a happy illusion.

Be watchful. If you see the clouds of temptation beginning to gather and form above your head, remember that the deceiver's plan is to steal. He wants to steal the gifts God already has given you by replacing them with something new, exciting, and faulty. It might look like a flock of enchanting birds circling above, but don't be deceived. Those are vultures. Satan wants you to believe that the old is useless, no longer important, and can be compromised. But there are some things you already have that God values. Now more than ever is the time to take inventory of what those things are.

Lastly, we should know that Satan is also called "the evil one," which comes from the Greek word *poneros*. *Strong's Dictionary* describes this as "hurtful...in effect or influence." In other words, he is out to impede our efforts in fighting the good fight of faith. He wants us to take our eyes off the bigger picture so that we recede and focus on the smaller picture—for instance, hurts and disappointments. As long as he can keep our view myopic, he will succeed at making us withdraw in the battle for what really matters.

Focusing on the smaller picture alters perception of value in the human heart. If all I can see is the hurt or wound I am feeling, I may forget that God has a greater purpose in the trial. We naturally tend to focus on the pain and all the details of the offense instead of on God's bigger picture.

Don't get me wrong. I know slights hurt. In fact, one of the things I hear the most from those who are going through a transition is that they feel invisible and slighted. I remember my own mother telling me this when she was in the transition of aging. Back then, it made me sad that she felt that way. Although I tried to understand, it wasn't until I came into this stage of life myself that I knew exactly what she meant.

In some sense, there is validity to this feeling. This is because in the younger seasons of life, we women are at the center of everything. If we have children, they see us as heroes. We are strong and in control. Whether in consumer marketing campaigns or in filling gaps in church ministries, we are the target age group that is recognized and sought after. Then, when we get older, we are no longer at the center. We stand on the fringes and watch the center shift. This is often when slights come into play. As our lives shift, Satan wants us to feel as though we are disappearing and simply don't matter anymore.

At this time, we must be watchful of the short-sighted view Satan desires us to have. After all, his lens is fixed to only focus us in on hurt and disappointment.

It's easy to see how this kind of afflicted thinking can form. For instance, consider John the Baptist's statement in regard to his disciples following after Jesus: "He must become greater; I must become less" (John 3:30). Upon reading this verse, if you are anything like me, you might feel a tinge of sadness for John, as if everything has shifted for him and he is disappearing. But then I comfort myself with the thought that it's Jesus who is becoming greater, so it's okay. Both these ideas are shortsighted. The phrase *He must become greater* didn't mean Jesus would become any greater in His being, because He was already greater. It meant, rather, that in the hearts of people, He would become greater—in fact, He would become their salvation, purpose, and reason for living. In a very real spiritual sense, John was becoming more, not less—there was a type of spiritual fullness happening in his heart. John was actually relaying a huge spiritual truth about his future—that while his circumstances were decreasing, his soul was expanding. His identity was actually solidifying in Christ. John saw the bigger picture of what really matters in this life and for eternity.

So it is with you and me. In Jesus, we are becoming more, not less. This is one of the most magnificent aspects of the exceptional bloom, and understanding and embracing the value of it causes our next season to take on a richer shade of color. A vivid reflection of Christ emerges inwardly, regardless of outward decline or circumstance. Standing on the outskirts is not a bad thing after all. Remember that Christ Himself was crucified outside the camp, and He calls us to join Him there. As Hebrews 13:13 (ESV) advises, "Let us go to Him outside the camp." He will safely lead us out of seasonal bubbles that inevitably vanish, to inward flourishing that endures forever.

God desires this for us. All the more reason to be watchful in all of these areas. We should be on high alert as we recognize that Satan will try to amplify our emotional state, cause breakdowns and divisions in our support systems, detour us with temptations and replacements, and convince us to focus on the smaller picture. Each one of these strategies is intended to impede the blooming that God has for flourishing in our next season.

Remember, as much as Satan would love for us to lose all hope by his charade of our demise, it is impossible for him to extinguish us. Why? Because our hope is set on royal blood.

I was amazed to discover after doing a little research that every single day we are alive, our bone marrow produces one billion stem cells that form the blood in our body. My goodness, I had no idea the process was so complex! The more I thought about it, the more I realized that in a similar manner, we often miss the complexity of the blood of Christ. Shouldn't we hold tightly, with greater depth of understanding, to the rescuing power found in the blood of Jesus? After all, this is our hope—or has it become more of an abstract notion that has lost its meaning? We can become accustomed to certain theological ideas such that after a time, they lose impact in our hearts. Rather than standing on the solid rock of truth, our hope gets blown around by our fluctuating emotions. What good is having an understanding of Satan's tactics if the one thing he targets—our hope in the restorative power of the blood of Jesus—fluctuates like the wind? Hope influenced by emotion can morph as we go through change. If we are feeling strong spiritually, our hope is strong, but when we are feeling weak, our hope is weak. This is why it is important to recognize that even though hope can stir our feelings, it should not be based on feelings.

Feelings can be extremely inconsistent, even

on a good day. Imagine how difficult it would be
for feelings to stay steady in an entire season of
uncertainty, such as transitional seasons in life. This
is why we need to grasp the certainty of a hope
in something that does not change, especially at a
time when there seems to be nothing in our lives
but change.

Hope in the original language of Scripture has
the meaning of confident expectation. It is a
stationary and fixed confidence in something that
is absolutely certain. This is when our faith moves
from an abstract idea to being our anchor. Ours is
a complete faith in the work accomplished on the
cross, outside of us and for us. Hope in anything
less than the blood of Christ, including some vague
"hopefulness," will be shaky at best. What we need
to know is this: Even if we lose hope, hope does not
lose us. Saving hope is not based on what we can
do or how we feel, but on what God has already
done by shedding His powerful blood for us.

This certainty is from God, who does not waver.

God does not go up and down. His perspective is
perfect at all times. He does not wake up in a bad
mood one day and a good mood the next. He is
constant and is always consistent. God is immutable
and never changes. He is holy and never differs
from this immutable state. There are no degrees or

shadows of turning in His being. Every one of His acts stems from His perfect and perpetual nature.

Our season of transition may experience turbulent shifting, but this will not alter God's never-changing position. Our purposes, goals, and directions will change, but His purposes will continue forever unchanged. If one day we feel secure and the next we are worried that our salvation is unsure, God's promise still stands true: "He chose us in Him before the foundation of the world" (Ephesians 1:4 ESV).

God is also infinite, unlike us. We are fragile creations, and everything about us is limited. God, however, is without limitation. His ways are boundless and immeasurable. God's capacity does not end. To say God's love is as wide as the ocean still conveys limits—therefore, we can only cry out, "God's love is unfathomable!" In our season of bloom, diving deep into the limitless bounties of His infiniteness causes our hearts to soar above our finite state. After all, our earthly bodies are simply temporary dwellings for our hearts, which are meant to enlarge with a limitless God.

God is sovereign. He is the highest authority there is. All creation and everything in it must answer to Him. No one is exempt. All earthly leaders will have to give account to Him. Here in our temporal realm, there are various social, cultural, and political orders. We often feel their structural pinch in our season of transition. Whatever situation you may find yourself in—whether it's being unseen, held back, oppressed, or mistreated by others, be assured that God has His eye keenly focused on you. Make no mistake about it—nothing happens without His complete knowledge. Eventually, the people who rise up against you will have to answer to God.

God is omnipresent, and you are never alone. This transitional season of life can bring on feelings of loneliness and isolation. For this reason, grasping this amazing attribute of God is a rich comfort to the soul. You are reassured of this remarkable truth in Psalm 139:

Where can I go from Your Spirit? Where can I flee from Your presence? If I go up to the heavens, You are there; if I make my bed in the depths, You are there. If I rise on the wings of the dawn, if I settle on the far side of the sea, even there Your hand will guide me, Your right hand will hold me fast. If I say, "Surely the darkness will hide me and the light become night around me," even the darkness will not be dark to You; the night will shine like the day, for darkness is as light to You. (Psalm 139:7–12)

If we lean into this reality, we will be greatly comforted. Sometimes we feel closer to God than at other times, but that doesn't change the fact that He is always there, regardless of how we feel. He doesn't distance Himself from us as we get older or go through transition. On the contrary, seasonal change invites us to draw closer to Him in heart and mind.

All this and more is our royal inheritance as daughters and sons purchased with an incomparable price: the blood of Christ. Through Him, we are of royal blood in the highest sense. In fact, every time Satan looks at us, he sees the blood of Christ marked on the doorposts of our hearts.

Oh yes, the work of Christ is complicatedly perfect and absolutely certain. Make no mistake about it—He paid a great price for us to have such a privileged and unshakable hope in something so rock solid! "But now in Christ Jesus you who once were far away have been brought near by the blood of Christ" (Ephesians 2:13). What a reassurance to realize that although our feelings about God may change, His feelings about us never change.

Therefore, let your soul rest as you recognize what an anchor you have in your God. It is such a marvel to consider that even in the midst of your ever-changing emotions and perspectives, especially seasons of difficulty, God never changes!

Although Satan, with his hope-stealing tactics, may try to impede our bloom, bloom we must! Even though we walk through the valley of the shadow of death—which is often what it feels like during the season of transition—we are not dead, as Satan would have us think. The truth is that we are walking in a unique space of time that is closer to heaven than we've ever been before, and it is God's desire to illumine this truth in a way that will thrill our souls! Therefore, let us cast off all weights that hold back our hope and move forward in prayer and faith.

Remember, though the vultures circle, you are not defeated. By the power of God, there is life in you, because Christ's life blood is upon you. It is certain!

EXCEPTIONAL BLOOM

Because the bromeliad has no roots and derives its nourishment from its leaves, its limbs have a fragile consistency and texture. Unlike other plants in our garden that are more resistant to impact, the bromeliad requires that we keep watch to prevent our big, clunky dog from snapping its growing leaves and petals.

5

A Time to Bloom

*I*t is often during the darkest seasons of life that we find ourselves welcomed by the most surprising shade of hope, like heavenly chiffon wrapping us in the beauty of an unexpected sunrise.

Having cast the vision, made divine evaluations, considered the process, and kept careful watch, now, my friends, we are at the finish line.

It is our time to bloom!

We have discussed in detail that life change and transition can be, at the very least, extremely disorienting. This still leaves us with the question, "Where is the silver lining?" It's one thing to talk about the blooming season ahead but quite another to experience it.

When does this shift occur?

Let me be frank in sharing that this period isn't about extinguishing suffering. The Bible tells us that there will be trials in life. And as we age, hardship will become more common. Billy Graham, in the introduction of his book *Nearing Home*, shares his thoughts on the subject: "All my life I was taught how to die as a Christian, but no one ever taught me how I ought to live in the years before I die." He goes on to say, "While the Bible doesn't gloss over the problems we face as we grow older, neither does it paint old age as a time to be despised or a burden to be endured with gritted teeth.... Nor does it picture us in our latter years as useless and ineffective, condemned to spend our last days in endless boredom or meaningless activity until God finally takes us home." Graham's transparency is refreshing. His recognition that aging was a season that had caught him off guard reveals a subject of much-needed dialogue. Honesty about the difficulties that come with transition in life is important because it brings a sense of validation and understanding. But along with these hard realities, somewhere in the midst of the pain of a new season, as a greater hope takes hold of our hearts, we will find the most enchanting of blooms if we allow Christ to show them to us.

This is how it happened for me.

One particular morning in a deep season of heartache, I awoke with a compelling urgency to pray. So, I prayed and opened my Bible to read. As I looked up from the pages, I saw the most magnificent tint of pink in the sky right outside my living room window. The pink wasn't simply in the sky but appeared to be all around—the air was thick with color. A remarkable joy swept over me, and I marveled at the shades of rose that seemed to permeate everything within my view. I burst outside to look more closely at this perfect glow that God had cast. It seemed as though I was being allowed to witness the presence of the kingdom at close range. In that moment, heaven intersected with the reality of my own little world, and if I didn't know any better, I would have thought I could leap from one world to the next with one simple step—like the heavens opened up to let me know there is more— and it is very, very good.

I was struck deeply. Pink—a color I once disregarded, was ushering in the dawning of a new season. And I thought to myself that if every other color were to disappear, somehow I would be okay. I felt an overwhelming sense of security encompass me as I considered what Christ had accomplished on the cross to make this happen. Hope transformed from concept to anchor for my soul. Oh, the certainty of it! I had done nothing to earn it, nor would I be able to do anything to lose it.

It was simply mine—freely. I marveled at the spiritual pink that branded itself in my heart at that moment. It was a fresh and powerful awareness of grace.

That was when the shift began.

Everything else—all the pain and disillusionment of life transition, all that was confusing, all that was failing, all that was fleeting, all that was my identity—would certainly fade like color washed out over time. This thought, set against the burgeoning rose hue that flooded my morning, highlighted two opposing realities—one diminishing, the other increasing. As I stood marveling at this juxtaposition, the pink beckoned me with fresh hope and comfort.

Up to this point, my mind had not grasped the potential of moving forward. Releasing attachments to the temporal had always been something to think about later, not something I thought about embracing in the present. This is because for most of my life, I had been young, and youthfulness has a way of pushing the idea of *letting go* into the future. However, all that changed in the twinkle of keen realization that the most vibrant shades of my own life already were dimming. I could see the slow fade. The woman I had been in my perceived prime—and my desperation to cling to that identity—was graciously being pried from my hands one finger at a time through pain and suffering. What was most astonishing was that God didn't just leave me standing there empty-handed. Instead, he held out vividly the most divine color of all: the color of grace, which never fades.

The color of grace—what a concept! Although I'm sure grace isn't really the color pink, somehow for me, this luminescent shade in the sky stamped a visual picture in my heart. This image not only remained, but it also began to glow more brilliantly the more I recognized and embraced it.

I have always considered pink to be a silly color that represents the unrealism of all things fluffy and frivolous. In fact, I was even quite a mocker of the color. I am more of a serious-natured soul and a realist, so pink just never seemed real or serious to me. During this season, however, it seemed more real and serious than anything I knew. It was like a banner that ushered my soul into a deeper dimension of truth.

It was my time to discover the rich beauty of who I am in Christ, which only would come from loosening my tight hold on those seasons in life that were naturally passing or had passed. All that I would let go of and allow to die and fall to the ground would blossom into a ravishing spiritual bloom. As John 12:24 says, "Very truly I tell you, unless a kernel of wheat falls to the ground and dies, it remains only a single seed. But if it dies, it produces many seeds." For me, this experience was, indeed, the crossover. I felt the roots of my identity in my life here on earth break free from the ground that day. The possibility of what might come next became an exciting prospect to consider.

I saw this transition reflected in my grandmother when I was a young girl. In her early adult years, she was endearingly cranky. But sometime after the age of fifty, something changed, and she began a gradual beautifying of the inner spirit as she continually dwelt upon "my sweet Jesus," as she called Him. The more she lost—or let go of—down here, the greater her grasp of the eternal became. She spoke about the kingdom of God, and she talked of how excited she was about being there some day. I didn't understand how she could talk that way, although I found it comforting when she did. To me, it seemed like she was closer to the angels because her heart was so richly planted in the clouds. In fact, the older she got, the lovelier she became, almost as if she were an angel herself.

Interestingly, the bromeliad bloom has the same extraordinary way about it. Its roots do not go into the ground to get nourishment, as is the case with most plants. Rather, the bromeliad draws in water through its leaves from the moisture in the air. In other words, this exceptional plant does not look downward for its strength but upward. Instead of dependence on earth for its sustenance, the bromeliad fervently seeks the heavens for its life. Life after transition offers the same opportunity. All the losses we have experienced actually force us not to look to our roots in the ground for strength—a source which previously formed our identity—but to look upward to heaven for our strength. We gain imperishable sustenance by looking above rather than below and by looking ahead rather than back at the past, as Colossians 3:2 so wonderfully describes: "Set your minds on things above, not on earthly things."

Stepping into this place of the heart gave me a tremendous sense of freedom and oddly, rest. There is peace that comes from such an ordering of the soul. The experience of discovering exceptional hope in the midst of heartache was almost like an agonizing illness after which death gives way to life, or a difficult labor that allows for a beautiful birth.

Yours is a new season, and all the pain that has led up to this point fades in its light. As Matthew 10:39 says, "Whoever loses their life for My sake will find it."

The book of Ecclesiastes teaches that there are

seasons designated for the various phases and stages of life. For instance, there is a time to be born and a time to die—a time to laugh and a time to cry. For people facing transition, it is no different. Change shakes our sense of security to the core. But here is the key: where our hearts take root or uproot during this time will determine the direction of the bloom.

A great example of the opposing pulls of the heart can be found in the account of the two sisters in the Bible. Whenever people hear the story of Mary and her sister, Martha, they immediately identify with one or the other of them. They assume their own personalities must fall into one category or the other. But may I suggest there is a little of both of them in all of us? In fact, the well-known particulars of Martha and Mary's characters may surface in us depending on the frame of mind we are in. There are times in life when we run around in administrative mode, with the things of this world weighing on our thoughts. There are other times when we realize we need to rest from the never-ending to-do list of life and just sit at the feet of Jesus. The transition period leading to the exceptional-blooming season is that unique and tranquil place of the heart where we allow the Martha in us to shift more substantially into Mary mode. But I must add a caveat here so there is no misunderstanding. Whether we are in Mary mode or Martha mode, God loves and adores us equally. While His love toward us remains steady, our attention sometimes shifts away from Him. Although both women were in the house with Jesus, only Mary was able to keenly perceive the kingdom of God at close range. Let's look at the passage of Scripture that describes this occurrence.

> As Jesus and His disciples were on their way, He came to a village where a woman named Martha opened her home to Him. She had a sister called Mary, who sat at the Lord's feet listening to what He said. But Martha was distracted by all the preparations that had to be made. She came to Him and asked, "Lord, don't You care that my sister has left me to do the work by myself? Tell her to help me!"

> "Martha, Martha," the Lord answered, "you are worried and upset about many things, but few things are needed—or indeed only one. Mary has chosen what is better, and it will not be taken away from her." (Luke 10:38–42)

Interestingly, the introduction gives Martha first billing. The author could have started by simply stating there were two sisters, one named Martha, and one named Mary. But Martha is the one who is initially identified with the home Jesus and His disciples visited.

The passage doesn't give us the details, but I bet Martha's house was something special. I can imagine a perfectly manicured entrance staging the front door. Inside, we find every detail perfectly attended to—even matching dinnerware (pink patterns of course) already set on the table. The curtains are stunningly frilled, and a lovely fragrance from fresh-cut flowers flows throughout the house.

I'm sure she was known as the Martha Stewart of her time.

Mind you, the pink I refer to in this illustration is my former take on the color. This is what pink used to mean to me—perfect presentations of a superficial nature. If we go with this take for a moment, there is something else to be said about pink: it is the color of every human heart to some degree. What I mean by the pink of the human heart is our need to perfectly present ourselves to the world. Martha's desire to impress was no different from anyone else's. In fact, it may even have been less in comparison to what people feel they need to live up to in this day and age. We are an image-driven society, and we all struggle with this in one way or another. For many of us, our identity was conditioned in us early on. We may remember times when we felt the pressure to measure up when we were children. These pressures follow us into adulthood and affect every area of our being and all of our choices in life: what we wear, what we drive, where we live, whom we associate with, which credentials we earn, which careers we choose, which schools we send our kids to, and which groups we get involved in. The list goes on.

I need to make a confession. I've never had a great desire for fancy styles. In fact, I've had to force myself to be more intentional with my wardrobe choices so as not to be an embarrassment. The truth is, I have had an aversion to fashion for as long as I can remember. This is especially odd considering that I grew up in one of the most frivolous cities in the country, surrounded by designer names and haute-couture fashion. But that's partly why I ended up the way I did. You see, it's so easy to spot an exaggerated, puffed-up identity in the hedonistic culture in the part of Florida where I live. The pomp associated with fashion is a turn-off. Those who "have" are considered socially desirable, and those who "have not" aren't. When I was growing up, I found that very distasteful. Think about it. Is a piece of fabric with a label on it a reason to be admired? Living in the midst of this culture, I associated the color pink with these shallow displays of extravagance. (Incidentally, most of the buildings and shopping malls in the city where I lived were pink.)

The pink I associate with the superficial speaks of the human need to find our identity in how we appear to others and to ourselves. This is Martha's pink, and we know it well. It's the stuff we want people to think we're made of, particularly in the Christian community. We quote Bible verses, theologies, authors, and spiritual platitudes in a way that casts us as being spiritually "in the pink." We want to run successful church programs and ministries. Our religious personas, presentations, and affiliations become our identities. Plenty of these types of Marthas make up the Church. In fact, I might be so bold as to say that the Church is made up entirely of Marthas who occasionally switch into Mary mode.

The superficial pink of the human heart can always be identified by its demands for priority in our lives. Such was the case with Martha. The passage says, "But Martha was distracted by all the preparations that had to be made" (verse 40). Notice the words *had to*. What made Martha feel like the event *had to* be a certain way? Also notice the word *distracted*. There it is—the demand for priority. Martha was unable to fully enjoy the once-in-a-lifetime privilege of having Jesus in her home. Why? Because she felt compelled to live up to the ideals she had set in her own mind, and they took first billing.

We all have seasons in our lives, and our identity in these seasons is very important to us. For some, that importance may be driven by joy, and for others, it may even be driven by obligation or guilt. But whether or not we like a particular season, how strongly it fuels our identities (compelling us) will reveal its ranking. For instance, I love being a grandmother—what an amazing and joyful season! But I must confess there are times when grand-mothering compels me to lose sight of everything else, including my own spiritual journey separate from being "Gammy."

A season is not a bad thing, it is rather the degree of hold a season has on us that determines whether or not we are in Martha mode. In other words, what grip does a particular role have on our identities? Do we feel like we won't have meaning without it? Do we put it above other things that are important?

Martha was completely oblivious to the hold that living up to what her own and others' expectations had on her. In fact, she appealed to Jesus to ask Mary to help her. After all, Martha was doing all of this for Jesus, right? Many times, we make the same mistake. We have spent our energy for *someone else's sake*, and now that the season has changed, our efforts are no longer appreciated. This can be the cause of a great deal of depression at this time of life.

It must have been a shock for Martha to receive Jesus's response regarding priority. Regardless of Martha's shock, we must be careful not to miss the grace-filled intentions of our Savior as He spoke to her. Jesus addressed Martha by saying her name twice—"Martha, Martha"—which is very significant. Have you ever seen a movie in which a character is dreaming, and he or she is awakened by a voice calling his or her name twice? It is the same idea. Jesus cared deeply for Martha. This wasn't a rebuke but a loving call to awaken her (for her soul's sake) out of her season of being consumed with her perceived identity. In essence, Jesus was calling her to take note of a new season awaiting, one that Mary already had entered. It would not be a season of pink ruffles and table centerpieces, but a season that would cast a genuine, divinely pink glow on her soul.

As was the case with Martha, our awakening to a new season of life is certainly pivotal to consider. After all, all seasons are fleeting, like bubbles that form, take shape, and eventually evaporate. And every earthly endeavor, from beginning to end of life, is its own bubble—meaning, it carries its own characteristics encompassing things like structure and hierarchy. This may include position or title, privilege or disadvantage, theology or philosophy, family or friends, etc. Often, it isn't until we are outside of a past bubble that we recognize other ways of being. For instance, a friend of mine who was demeaned at her workplace for years only realized the extent of unhealthiness in that bubble when she acquired a favorable position in another company. Being demeaned had become so normalized that she didn't fully understand how different life could be until she was outside of that bubble.

In another example, a successful businessman whose wife left him became incapacitated with grief. When he realized his emotional and mental health were in peril, he sought the help of his local pastor. This pastor wisely offered him a temporary live-in service position in a homeless shelter. The businessman agreed and immersed himself in this opportunity. While there, he found himself connecting to wonderful people facing extreme forms of hardship. In witnessing their gratitude over simple acts of kindness, he was moved. Outside the bubble of his own grief, he was able to come alive again with fresh hope and new eyes.

We survive in some bubbles, while we thrive in others. My husband talks about our early years in marriage and family as Camelot years. It was an enchanting seasonal bubble of time. Yet, transitioning to grandparenthood was just as captivating in a new way. But notice—the prior bubble had to change for the next one to be experienced.

Martha was in her own bubble, and it stood in contrast to Mary's desire to sit at Jesus's feet. Martha attempted to wrangle Mary into her idea of how she thought hosting Jesus should look. Yet, Mary was not interested in this temporal distraction that would take her attention from Jesus. Meanwhile, Martha did not recognize that she was being given an opportunity through Mary to open her heart to what *true* hospitality looked like outside her limited bubble.

Strong's Dictionary describes the Greek word for "hospitality" found in First Peter 4:9, *philoxenos*, as "fond of guests." It is a tender quality toward the guest, paying careful attention. It implies a tuning in to the person who is the subject of your hospitality, understanding and anticipating their needs. It doesn't strive—instead, it sits and leans in. Listening, therefore, would be an essential identifying characteristic of true hospitality. This is what we find with Mary.

An illustration from one of my daughters, who is married to the pastor of a small church, gives further insight. She shares a story about a dinner invitation she and her husband received. It was from a couple—very nice people and members of the church. When my daughter and her husband walked in the door, the emphasis on presentation was so evident that they actually felt uncomfortable sitting on the furniture. This set the course for stiff movement throughout the evening. Not wanting to make a mess or interrupt the host's flow, my daughter stayed alert to the surroundings to meet the expectation for the occasion. The funny thing was that these people were eager and truly wanted to display hospitality. Yet, unbeknownst to them, they made their guests feel ill at ease. The hosts did not realize that their focus on *all that had to be done* (as in the case with Martha) put their guests in the position of catering to the hosts' anticipations.

Unfortunately, the host and hostess, in the effort to impress their guests, missed out on the truest sense of hospitality, which is simply to tune in, pay attention to their guests' needs, and make them feel comfortable.

How did what they really wanted to accomplish go so awry?

The truth is, most of us desire to make the right

choices and go in the right directions but just don't know how to get there.

My husband gave me a good word picture to describe this. He said it is like being on a ship headed toward the brave new world. And we see it—this new Eden—right in front of us. It is the land of all we can be in Christ. But we stay in the familiar old ship, and we don't disembark.

This is also the case when it comes to transition. We get tripped up, hanging on to how we have always done life. We are flooded with feelings that have accompanied these seasons. We don't know how to move forward. Yet, transition provides an opportunity for an awakening to a new direction— one that has its roots above and not below. In His tenderness toward Martha's inability to get there, Jesus lovingly revealed that she must loosen her grip on the temporal in order to make room for the spiritual. One was a passing, seasonal bubble of time, while the other held eternal implications. Mary made the better choice and it would not be taken from her. While Martha's "pink" was about appearances and the expectations of a hostess, Mary experienced the genuine pink glow of God's grace. Mary knew where she belonged—near Jesus—and she drank in all that He had for her. She sat at His feet, in the position of a disciple humbly learning from her Teacher. She may have appeared to others to be lazy or neglectful of the tasks of a hostess. But her identity was found in her nearness to God and all that He was able to pour into her because of her attentive listening. Martha was invited do the same.

What about you?

Jesus has already given you permission to loosen your grip on the *many things to be worried or upset about*. Maybe it's time to give yourself permission.

You don't need to expect so much of yourself.

You don't need to fulfill other people's expectations.

You don't have to solve everything.

You don't have to have it all figured out.

It's okay to make mistakes.

It's okay if others make mistakes.

It's okay not to be perfect.

It's okay for others not to be perfect.

It's okay if someone doesn't like you.

It's okay not to agree.

It's okay to let go of regret.

It's okay to slow down.

It's okay to get older.

It's okay to cry.

It's okay to laugh.

It's okay to relax.

We must also loosen our grip on how we thought life should be. This is not easy because it requires yielding to something that feels very strange to us. Letting go of our aspirations goes against treasured hopes. There is death involved—death of a dream, an ideal. Life-altering events like death, divorce, violation, sickness, job loss, and natural disasters are traumatic. Sometimes we are flanked with such sadness we feel unable to let go, as if loosening our grip means giving up on important dreams or memories. Often, we hang on emotionally as a way of attending to and guarding them. Yet, A. W. Tozer, in his book *The Pursuit of God*, shares an important realignment: "We are often hindered from giving up our treasures to the Lord out of fear for their safety.... Everything is safe which we commit to Him, and nothing is really safe which is not so committed."

Remember, God already knew you would face these losses. He can be trusted with their outcomes and your brokenness. They are safer in His hands than they are in yours. Meanwhile, He invites you to move forward in a new way.

The truth is, our stories don't end with the temporal losses and changes we face. All that we were and all the pain we have gone through are certainly *part* of God's story for our lives. But they are not the whole story—our story is still unfolding.

Perhaps you have become aware of this paradox

in your own life. You can see two directions set before you. On the one hand, you are consumed with thoughts of your earthly identity and how you long for it to look or how it used to be. That vision is set against the enthralling thought of your identity in Christ and how beautiful it really can be. There is such a sense of warmth and freedom in stepping forward with Jesus. For the woman facing this exceptional-blooming season, a defining moment occurs when she goes from trying to hold on to being the fading princess in one story to recognizing that she is emerging as a queen in another.

Jesus's call—"Martha, Martha"—is His call to all of us. Ladies, this is our story—the one that begins with "Once upon a time..." Imagine the grand doors of destiny swinging open as we enter the most fabulous of season of our lives. The path strewn with pink rose petals has led us to the season closest to heaven.

We are brides being readied for the most enchanting of wedding days. Our attention to bridal details will become more heightened as the grand event approaches. Our hearts will begin to soar with Mary-like anticipation of our beloved Groom, the Man of our dreams.

Let me tell you a little something about this Man. It is His desire for you to come alive to Him as never before. It is your time not to simply know

His feelings toward you but also to believe them in the deepest part of your heart. He sees you as His spotless bride washed as white as snow. Nothing you ever have done wrong is held against you. Nothing you do in the future will be held against you. Any failures and sins are gone from His sight. You are not an afterthought but His treasured choice. He will never criticize you or find fault in you. He isn't waiting for you to improve. He loves you fully, even though He knows everything about you. In His presence, you are highly honored and valued. *Lean in* as He whispers to your heart, "Rise up, My love, My fair one, and come away" (Song of Solomon 2:10 NKJV). This is your truest identity. You are God's beloved. Like Mary, you are choosing "what is better," and it will not be taken away from you.

If you have felt beaten up from the disappointments of this world, from loss, or from failed expectations, Jesus is waiting to bind your wounds and adorn you in royal attire. Won't you allow Him to clothe your soul?

He offers you a garment of strength. When you step into it you become strong and secure because your heart's roots are reaching upward. You possess a security that others vividly sense. Even the younger generation marvels and wants to be around you. You realize that all they have will fade someday too, so you become the voice of wisdom they long to hear.

Add to this the covering of the Spirit. Finding your soul drenched in His Word, overflowing in refreshing measure, you are filled and complete. That's right—even youthfulness doesn't come close to the enlivening force that manifests at this time.

Then there's the cloak of patience, which so warmly wraps the heart as you detach more and more from the exasperating demands of life's expectations. Such softness comes with this gentle change. Lovely and gracious to be around, you become a breath of fresh air in a tightly wound world.

A raiment of clarity is draped across your shoulders in this season, and you wear it well. Although your eyesight may dim, your spiritual vision becomes wonderfully clear, and you are able to see things in ways you previously never considered. You finally can smell the roses because you can see them now. Small and simple things take on great value. You now find humor in issues that once unnerved you.

Amazingly, you are becoming the woman described in Proverbs 31:25–26, which states, "She is clothed with strength and dignity; she can laugh at the days to come. She speaks with wisdom, and faithful instruction is on her tongue." You are beginning a new phase of life, one in which the beauty of this blooming only increases. This is not simply a silver lining, but a special and divine season all its own. Dare I even say that it is the pinkest of times! It is inwardly lovelier, like "my sweet Jesus." "Therefore we do not lose heart. Though outwardly we are wasting away, yet inwardly we are being renewed day by day" (Second Corinthians 4:16).

Being renewed day by day sounds like something pricy that should come in a fancy bottle. This is a reminder straight out of Scripture that something very special and beautiful happens inwardly when we set our affections on Christ, no matter how old we are or how many transitions we face. It is the exceptional-blooming season before the ultimate bloom of being in heaven itself. It is a unique sliver of time on earth that intersects with the kingdom of heaven at closest range.

Now, when we consider some of the possibilities we discussed in chapter 1, we can face them with a new perspective. What are those things we have always wanted to do but never got around to? We now have time to pursue the talents God has given us to explore. Now, more than ever, we can appreciate the beauty of travel—even a trip around the block yields new wonder. Maybe there's a book, a movie, a topic of study, or a project that inspires you, and now you are ready to dive into it fully.

God is doing a new thing in your life. How

perfectly God works through casting the vision, divinely evaluating, undergoing the process, and keeping watch in preparing our hearts. They are all a part of the journey that brings us to a particular place in the soul, a divine turning point, a time to bloom. Now we are able to embark upon these new adventures with a new skip in our step. It is one thing to try to ease grief with fun activities but quite another to enjoy life because you're excited about what lies ahead as you move forward with God.

Adventure is no longer an idol in our hearts or the pursuit of another source of happiness to anesthetize us against pain. Instead, adventure becomes a pleasurable experience in a heart gripped by the love of God. In other words, life no longer grips us; God grips us so that we can enjoy life.

Satan's attempts to keep you far from this turning point of the soul will fall flat. Be assured that although he brings on full-scale attacks at this most vulnerable time in your life, he cannot extinguish your bloom because its roots have no place in his dominion. He is defeated, and ultimately, he will lose. The blackness of vultures in the sky must give way to the pink splendor of a new day.

And yes, the bloom of our old house finally arrived! It became one of the most beautiful homes in the neighborhood—even better than when it was brand new more than fifty years ago. Keep in mind that this old house could not fix itself. It had to rely on something outside of itself for renewal—and renewal it received!

My prayer, dear friend, is that if God somehow has brought this book across your path, He is in the process of revealing His exceptional bloom in your heart. Make no mistake about it—He has been preparing the way all along. Cross over, if you will, and experience the most magical time of your life. It is the exceptional bloom of flourishing in the next season.

EXCEPTIONAL BLOOM

Like the bromeliad, you are no ordinary design. God always intended your roots to spring upward for strength and nourishment. Only then can the exceptional bloom of your new season open to its fullest splendor, vibrantly displayed in divine shades of pink. Your beauty is truly matchless, for God has dipped your unique bloom in His amazing grace.

About the Author

PAULA MASTERS is a married mother of five grown children and grandmother of eleven who resides in Florida, where she manages overfiftyandfab.com/next.html, a faith-based online publication encouraging women to flourish in the "NEXT" season of life.

Acknowledgements

I thank my Lord and Savior, Jesus Christ, who has inspired me in ways that only He could.

Thank you to my sweet husband, who has not only been my anchor but is my biggest fan. He is my best friend, my love, and my life partner, who supports my desire to write the things on my heart.

I thank my five adult children for inspiring me by who they are. My daughter Kristin, who is gracious beyond words, brims over with exceptional wisdom and has supported me at every turn. She believes the best in people and gives them wings to soar. My daughter Abby, who is marvelously driven, richly kind, and ministry minded, inspires me with her initiative to get things done. I have mirrored much of my life's structure and discipline after her fine example. My daughter Ali, who is wonderfully creative, free-spirited, and strong, inspires and captivates me with her smile and charming ways. I love to watch her creations take masterful shape. My daughter Darbi, who is amazingly ambitious, determined, and a communication wizard. She is a deep thinker with a great gift of influence. I am awed at her abilities to be a mover and shaker in this life. And my artsy youngest, Teddy, who is uniquely spirited and full of life and fills the world with wonder, personality, and presence.

Last but not least are my eleven precious grandchildren—Grace, Aliyah, Maxwell, Charlie, Auggie, Oliver, Vanny, Henry, Gabby, Essie, and Arthur—who are responsible for filling my heart with the greatest joy!

Made in United States
Orlando, FL
01 June 2023

33694598R00071